Reflections on
Proverbs of My Seasons

"In Proverbs of my Seasons, the voice of poet Pat Stanford rings clear. A longing for love and a yearning for answers fill her poems with haunting words that stay with you as though lyrics of a particularly poignant song. Spring shows us love, both won and lost. Summer lets us into the hearts of friends, tried and true or fair-weather. Autumn sings of change, when what we know can become something entirely different. Winter brings memories of youth when happiness was sometimes elusive, and despair was not yet a part of the song."

—Lyla Faircloth Ellzey
*Peregrination, the
Poetry of Travel*

"I have tried to write about love. Pat Stanford captures its sweet agony in the poem "Key to my Heart." I have thrown away the key. When I was a young man, love was a lark. Pat Stanford sees. Old socks are more than simple comfort. I'll kill you later . . . when it's really good. Two poems that tell me how I've felt. To try and understand, take each and every stanza in your hand, and taste it. Pat Stanford makes me want to believe."

—Dee Christensen II
Even Bad Poetry is Good

"Our modern society has been criticized for not honoring life's many transitions with sufficient ceremony. Transitions are often limited to birth, graduation, marriage, and death, but we undergo so many more events in our lives. They also mark gradual changes in our emotions, personal growth, and shifts in our perspective about things from the grand to the mundane. Pat has created ceremony with her poems, honoring her transitions. Using rhyme and rhythm she provides insight into one woman's seasons."

—Linda Whitefeather
Cats Speak (feline poetry)

Proverbs of My Seasons
Poetry of Transition

Pat Stanford

DocUmeant *Publishing*
244 5th Avenue
Suite G-200
NY, NY 10001
646-233-4366
www.DocUmeantPublishing.com

Published by
DocUmeant Publishing
244 5th Avenue, Suite G-200
NY, NY 10001

646-233-4366

Copyright ©2019 Pat Stanford. All rights reserved

Limit of Liability and Disclaimer of Warranty: The design, content, editorial accuracy, and views expressed or implied in this work are those of the author.

No part of this publication may be reproduced, stored in a retrieval system, or transmitted in any way by any means—electronic, mechanical, photocopy, recording, or otherwise—without the prior permission of the copyright holder, except as provided by USA copyright law.

For permission contact the publisher at:
Publisher@DocUmeantPublishing.com

Cover Design by: Babski Creative Studios
Layout & Illustrations by: Ginger Marks
DocUmeant Designs
www.DocUmeantDesings.com

Library of Congress Control Number: 2019933058

ISBN13: 978-1-9378-0198-4 (10.99 USD)

Contents

Introduction vii

PART ONE: SPRING

Key to My Heart 3
Lonely Road 4
Touched by Love 5
Solitary Question 6
It Wasn't Bad 7
It's So Hard 8
The Survivor 9
Only Love 10
Love is Like an Old Sock 11
Afterglow 12
How It Used to Be 13
Love of the Loved 14
Things Not Said 15
A Retrospect 16
I'm So Tired 17
The Error 18
Phantom 19
The Two of You 20
Air for a Flute 21
Phantom II 22
Moody Like Me 23
The Sigh 24
Temporary Insanity 25
First, You Cry 26
Fall in Love 27
Lighthouse 28
Goodbye 29

PART TWO: SUMMER

Carry On, Regardless 33
Prospecting Friends 34
A Best Friend is Forever 35
Death of a Friendship 36
Verse to a Friend 37
Always Third 38
If I Laugh 40
Don't Bother Me 42
Happy Birthday to a Friend 43
I'll See You in My Dreams 44
To One Who Inspired 46
Iron Lady 47
Desolation 48
On Survival 50
In Appreciation 51
To Susan 52
River 53
Broken Arrow 54
A Patch of Briars 55
Trinity 56
Dark Side of the Moonchild 57
Duck Shit Sunday 58

PART THREE: AUTUMN

Paths 63
The Undefeated Ocean 64
Destiny 65
Night Harbor 66
Painting of a Storm 67
Storm at Sea 68
Serenity 69
Early in the Morning 70
Sky Beasts 71
Tragedy 72

Souvenirs 74
The Lonely Traveler 75
To Evening. 76
In Memoriam 77
Keep On Growing 78
The Park. 79
Ode to a Canary 80
Destiny of Frogs 81
Sunday Morning Tragedy 82
The Fiend 84
Sleeping Earth 85
Boomerang 86
The New Season 87
The View from the Porch .88
Uncomfortable Repose 89
Patterns 90

PART FOUR: WINTER

A Lifetime 93
An Old Song 94
Wisdom of Water 95
Mountain of Truth 96
Woodard's Garden 97
Alone in the Dark 98
I Looked Away 99
I'm Going to Neptune 100
Life in a Goldfish Bowl .101
Old Woman of the Road 102
Prophesy 103
Silence 104
My Soul and the Wind. .105
Drift Away 106
Like Dreamers Do 108
After Work 109
The Savage 110
Graduation 111

Beware the Grapevine 112
Memories 113
Paper 114
Fighting the Same War 115
Island in the Sun 116
Pipe Dreams 117
Poetry 118
The Child 119
Ascension 120
Pulitzer. 121
Advent 122

Acknowledgments 123

Additional Works by Pat Stanford 127

Introduction

I have been writing poetry practically since I could first hold a pencil. It always just seemed natural to me. My mother had several of those little clothbound write-in books filled with her poems. They were mostly simple little ditties, but she still had fun with them and wrote them, matching the ink color to the color of the cover. That is what poetry is to me — just having a bit of fun with words. I never laid claim to being a "serious" poet and I doubt mine are "for the ages" yet there are a few gems here, so say friends.

Much of my poetry rhymes because I like the added challenge, and the fact that many of them came to me as songs back when I could still play the guitar. (Lopping off a fingertip stopped my career as a troubadour.) Most appear in quatrains, couplets, or similar formats, because that is the influence that most stuck with me, although I have been stretched a little by several local poetry groups where we explored new and obscure forms. I most like writing "off the cuff" as we sometimes do in our meetings, but I always go back and "mess with them" some more, simply because I can't help myself.

Here, I present thoughts on many topics written throughout my "seasons" of life. Some thoughts have changed along with those seasons and I may no longer embrace what was written in the same way. Rather than destroy some poems, I either left them totally alone to remind me how far I have progressed since they were first conceived or have edited them to be more contemporary.

I sincerely hope you enjoy this collection.

Fair warning: I have more.

Spring

A Warm Glow of Hearts
Love — real or imagined is equal in its surmised glow

Key to My Heart
Lonely Road
Touched by Love
Solitary Question
It Wasn't Bad
It's So Hard
The Survivor
Only Love
Love is Like an Old Sock
Afterglow
How It Used to Be
Love of the Loved
Things Not Said
A Retrospect
I'm So Tired
The Error
Phantom
The Two of You
Air for a Flute
Phantom II
Moody Like Me
The Sigh
Temporary Insanity
First, You Cry
Fall in Love
Lighthouse
Goodbye

Key to My Heart

Inside of me, deep down therein,
love was locked inside my heart;
kindness wouldn't pry it; sighs wouldn't move it,
yet it was always there from the start.

Once, my soul grew so lonely
that it crept out; slowly came to show
itself on the surface for all to see,
but they did not care or want to know.

Then, all the pain and hurt it suffered
made it retreat further into me.
So, I doubled the chains, locked the locks,
and then threw away the key.

Lonely Road

You said, "I love you, will you marry me?"
though it was long ago, I remember it well.
Now you run from your weekend wives
like a scorched bat out of Hell.

What have I done that you turn me away;
why did love die after so few years?
What did you love then, that you don't love now;
why don't you ever tell me your fears?

Life's lonely roads are yet lonelier still,
knowing your loving thoughts aren't of me.
At times, I think hard of the day I'd leave,
and how I'd live alone, being totally free.

Your soft brown eyes have grown hard;
they used to say, "I love you so."
Without a single word spoken,
I knew love would continue to grow.

I'm frightened by our love's end as
the life we now lead seems so very fake.
What should we do—cast it all away;
sell the home we worked hard to make?

I still need you, I still want you.
Isn't there anything at all we can do?
I don't want a divorce, or move away,
so, I walk my lonely road, with you.

Touched by Love

As I touch you and you touch me,
   I wonder what it's like to be
     touched by love.

We make love, always in the dark,
   and it's only for a lark—
     not with love.

I hear snores from you instead of sighs;
   you don't know how my heart dies
     for your love.

You seem so damn well satisfied,
   only when we're physically unified,
     and not by love.

Once we were close, I saw your eyes
   on me through the night, 'til sunrise.
     Then we both knew love.

Now that's been so long ago
   and I'd really like to know
     what it was like to be . . .
       touched by love.

Solitary Question

Will I become overbearing when we marry
or take your love for granted?
Will I expect things I'd never dare
   expect from my best friend?

Will my mind start to wander to others
who may seem more beautiful or handsome;
and will you feel alone and hurt,
   and yet, happiness pretend?

Will I seek to own or cage you?
Will I drive you to someone else;
and misunderstand
   why you'd ever leave?

Will I beg you to come back to me;
when will you say you never will,
and that our love died sooner
   than I could ever believe?

It's my solitary question
before we go down the aisle;
it'll hurt less now and take less time
   if we talk it out for a while.

It Wasn't Bad

What we had was not too much;
you never gave a gentle touch.
Real communication, we never had,
other than that, it wasn't bad.

You said "Why I drink, I do not know,
it's just another place to go."
When you come down, you look so sad,
despite all that, it wasn't bad.

So much about you, I didn't know,
we didn't give each other room to grow.
Our relationship was a passing fad—
if that's all it was, it wasn't bad.

A common need to fulfill
one or the other's crazy thrill . . .
I lived each day a "love nomad"
so, for a gypsy's life, it wasn't bad.

But now I look back on that life,
as I steadily sharpen the knife;
while I'm ending it now, I'm not sad,
and I'd have to say, that it wasn't bad.

It's So Hard

Because I speak my mind, the feelings always shatter.
If that's the way you feel, then time won't really matter.
You say I'm impatient about relationship's development;
truth be told, I just look forward to good times being spent.

I know what I believe in—I believe in honesty;
"walking on eggshells" has no place with me.
So careful with your words, can't you speak your mind?
If you're not man enough to talk, I don't need your kind.

And what begins to happen to you and your career
may not have me in the picture in the coming year.
I may want to move on and to build up my view,
while you must remain here—your choices are few.

I know it's hard for you to see it this way,
but our education differs like night and day.
I'll always want more while you've got twelve years
You feel I'll outdo you, that's one of your fears.

It's hard for two people to always stay close
without one or the other feeling morose,
so, I'll take my wildest dreams and continue on,
to have time to think, breathe, sing my own song.

The Survivor

Your devotion to me is tempting, but,
I don't understand—for it's been so long.
You say you love me when I'm far away,
why not before, if the feelings were strong?

I never felt different, 'til now, I guess.
Then, I thought of you only as a friend,
Should I now feel more for you because
you're more intense with each card you send?

I guess I felt like one hell of a heel
because I don't feel the same as you;
perhaps it's because we're so far apart . . .
I don't think so—I thought it all through.

What did I do to make you feel this way—
or am I the play on your old love's rebound?
It is just the way it looks to me right now;
let's back off and not run it in the ground.

You say, "If you're the same as I knew in school,
then I could love you forever so true."
Well, I went on to more progressive things
and grew up since then—didn't you?

In all my travels, I've met many new friends
who have expanded my arbitrary views;
I've survived losing many unnecessary things,
so, I'll survive losing another man like you.

Only Love

If I can love you as I do now
without being there with you,
and I only know a small part of you
that makes up the whole...
If I can say the things I want to
in a letter or on the phone
and I know I'm not exaggerating
when I speak what's in my soul...

If I can battle feelings of insecurity
and still, you stay right there,
and when I'm thinking of you,
there's nothing I want to conceal...
If I know a comfort level with you
that I share with no one else,
then we have for a lifetime
only love, deep and sweet, to feel.

Love is Like an Old Sock

Love is like an old sock—
it gives you comfort, yes indeed!
You can wear it all the time,
not just when there is a need.

When love gets full of holes,
after quarrels rip it to the core,
you darn it back together
and it's stronger than before.

Love is wool and coziness
when it's all brand spankin' new,
but it gets battered down and matted
from years of hard use from two of you.

It should always be machine washable
and low heat tumble dry.
Happiness comes from careful use,
and on that, you can rely!

Afterglow

Your eyes meet mine again
and this time, I see you deep;
we look at each other exhausted,
yet, neither of us wants to sleep.

You kiss me in the afterglow—
a warmth that comes from within;
a moment before, you were far away,
and I'd wondered where you'd been.

This is a velvet moment
when we marvel in each other's care,
with each heartbeat felt in the silence,
each movement, watched as we stare.

We want this closeness to never end
but we both know that it soon will,
so, we breathe in deep and cherish
this moment, warm and still.

How It Used to Be

Just because it's dark
and I can't see the picture on the wall
which was made when we were happy,
doesn't mean I can't see how it used to be.

And because the only light
is from the clock, saying it's three a.m.
I stare at it, because I can't sleep
for thinking of how it used to be.

Soon that damned old alarm
will assault my ears and stop your snores.
You'll stumble to the bathroom to shave,
while I remember how it used to be.

I smile, staring at the dark ceiling
listening, awaiting morning's arrival,
and it won't take long for me to say to you,
"That's all for you and me, and how it used to be."

Love of the Loved

When love is real, it doesn't cling,
tie you down, enslave you or sting.
The heart knows when there is room to grow,
and freedom to move, to love and let go.

If there's love enough to set you free,
there's freedom to return when you both agree.
To be happy and peaceful, love needs to roam;
if there's plenty of room, love always comes home.

Allow for growing pains, let them always be felt;
start smothering love, soon it will melt.
Encourage deep feelings, then love comes to you.
Don't overshadow love—it knows what to do.

When love is real, look at what the eyes say—
about feelings they hold and don't look away.
If you set love free and it doesn't return,
then it never was yours, as soon you will learn.
To see the love of the loved reflected in one's eye,
you must give and take, then it never will die.

Things Not Said

In the silence between us, in things not said,
we are drifting apart, not growing. Instead,
from the lack of honesty, lack of reply
to the void that never fills, we wonder why.

Is it me not listening, or is it you
not pointing out your point of view?
Why are you so afraid of what's in my head?
Why are we missing the things not said?

Who are we kidding, how deep does it hurt
in conversation so clever, so sly, so curt?
So, when we look back on this before we are dead,
will we leave in our *will*, the things not said?

A Retrospect

I will never, ever know why
but I have wanted to make you cry;
to cut into you so very deep,
then sit back and watch you weep.

Am I there in your dreams of fortune;
am I there when you are only a bum—
what are you thinking of me right now,
or is not showing yourself rule of thumb?

You are, sometimes in the best of my dreams,
and sometimes you're not there at all.
Does this mean I don't feel the same for you;
is this the lull before the massive fall?

Yes, I want to cut deeply into you,
not only to make you bleed,
but to drain your pent-up feelings,
to know them—I still have a need.

I'm So Tired

Will I ever touch your heart
or will we stagnate on this tier?
If truth of my love cannot impart
to you, how can I make it clear?

I seek you, but never will I find
a key to unlock all that is in
your secretive, indifferent mind.
I pray it's not an awful, deadly sin.

Years have passed, and you've not grown
out of concern for your prosperity goal.
What are you saying when you don't speak;
what lies deep, unsung in your soul?

You say I go on and on about trust,
and how a love relationship should be.
Yet, I'm so tired of trying to show you
that all I can do now is set you free.

 The Error

You never said you loved me, nor I, you,
so, how did either of us know what was true?
Now, I'm the one who feels like a fool;
returning someone's love is the general rule.

On the beach with soft breezes, the surf and your child,
your reaction to my admission was surprisingly mild.
Then you asked what was wrong, as though concerned.
Tell me how you'd feel if your love had been spurned?

I guess you know that feeling—you've been married;
but it was more of a great burden that you carried.
You once asked, "What's emotion—overwrought tears?"
I think you'd like to conquer it just to cover your fears.

I made a mistake in thinking you had changed,
that you were wiser now and had life all arranged;
what of your error—one you've not seen yet—
say three words I must hear—how droll can you get?

Phantom

I think of you most of the time—
I've been in love with you for years.
I only wish that soon we'd meet;
before my love for you disappears.

I don't know where to find you
nor, to what ends I must go
to know you, touch and hold you;
how long it'll be before I know.

I've set you as my standard,
the man I'll wait years to find;
I don't need to draw a picture,
your image is rooted in my mind.

Mediocrity and half-finished things
are not a part of what you are.
You set your course and head for it
and doubtless you'll go far.

Considerate in all the things you do
and a sense of humor to lift you high,
your presence in a circle of friends,
will only good things for them magnify.

Why is it that I can't find you?
Could it be as though it seems
that you are not a man of flesh and blood—
only a phantom of my dreams?

The Two of You

One of you is passion, full of love and life;
the other, angry at it all, mostly at your ex-wife.
But whisky unbinds your tie, then your feelings.
You pour out tales of deep hurts and dirty dealings.

Without alcohol's magic, you are not free—
in daylight, a house cat is all you seem to be.
You show a different side, later in the night,
when a tiger emerges, with a lover's appetite.

I wanted the tiger, instead he began purring
and I couldn't keep that from occurring.
So, now which of the two, really is you?
I want to know that before we are through.

Air for a Flute

Unexpressed love is like singing a song
in a boundless void, heard by no one.
The sound is quite beautiful, expansive,
yet is lost forever to oblivion.

I surprised you with an aria
on a day I felt free to sing;
we never got past the overture—
you were a violin with a broken string.

You are not a violin—more like a flute,
flittering, fluttering and dashing around;
you can't commit yourself to the cadenza
and you'd never play a somber sound.

At times, you appear as a section
of instruments playing as one.
Other times, you wander off a note,
leaving unfinished what you've begun.

Freedom of the flute suits you well,
but at times you're not always there;
to express a passionate, dreamy piece,
yet for a flute, you could supply the air.

Phantom II

I realized why you are the one for me
recently when someone said "goodbye."
With no questions asked, you were there
even in times when I needed to cry.

You're always in love with me, it never fails—
we can always work things out with a smile,
then frolic like children on a sunny day
enjoying each other's company all the while.

I know you're not real, but I still want you
and no one ever has to know,
so should I continue on with a ghost—
a figment of dreams—or let you go?

Moody Like Me

We'll kill each other before we're through;
you leave me now, and later, I leave you.
We take turns heading toward the door,
or play nasty games to even the score.

One day we're happy, the next we're sad;
I leave you angry, you leave me mad.
We've got to end this, don't you see?
You're a fickle love—moody like me.

Go find someone who tends to your beck and call,
I think that's what you want dear, after all.
I won't abandon my desire to see all in life,
refuse to be tied down, so I can't be your wife!

Let's call it all off now, let's please cut the line
since I can't be yours and you can't be mine.
We can still be friends, on that we can agree
it won't work Babe, you're moody like me.

The Sigh

Some can't do a thing for you;
yet they don't really know why.
Some can't simply say, "I love you,"
and unintentionally make you cry.

Where are the men Anne Murray sings of?
They are so different and self-assured.
Or is she a dreamer, just like me,
singing about something totally absurd?

How long must I know you, what do I say,
and will it make a difference when I do?
I loved you once and spoke those words
but how did you react to "I love you?"

Did you say, "Oh really, do you now?"
and pass it off with some gauche remark,
or did you want to take my hand
and like old times, stroll the park?

Sometimes I want you so much I can't stand it,
sometimes I don't want you at all.
Sometimes I want to tell you how I feel,
sometimes I wish you'd never call.

Life's a journey, they say, leading to love,
well we've been through a lot, does that qualify?
I know you, yet I don't—I'll be with you, yet I won't.
The teeter-totter that is us, brings a sigh.

Temporary Insanity

When it's good, it's really good,
but more and more it just isn't so;
people now don't want to work things out
or give one another room to grow.

Love should be a flower that sprouts,
not a facade for one person's vanity;
and all the more, I think it's so—
it's just temporary insanity.

You come, you go—you leave, you stay,
and hurt me without caring or knowing.
Your mood changes almost every day,
depending on the way the wind is blowing.

I have to leave this crazy cycle now,
I can't take another attack on my humanity;
you can keep your concept of what is truth,
claiming that it was all temporary insanity.

First, You Cry

I went to see a friend of mine
who'd moved to another town.
We'd spent many years together,
before our moving all around.

She'd had a little girl,
now about thirteen.
She started asking questions
and seemed so very keen.

Asking me instead of her mom,
because I didn't pose a threat
about dreams of love and marriage.
I was startled and began to sweat.

I said, "First you cry a lot,
and when you can weep no more
he'll either stay and love you
or he'll head out for the door."

Fall in Love

Just as when you fall in love
and notice all the love songs
you too, will notice all of those
about love dying or its wrongs.

Just as when you fall in love
and feel the claw that grips your chest
you'll feel that same claw's grip
when the love is laid to rest.

Various degrees of emotion
make you happy when you should be
and make you sad when you should not,
yet it all feels the same to me.

So why bother to fall in love
when all it does is bring anxiety?
Run around with all that inside
so your life will have some variety.

If you never bother to fall in love
both sides you'll never see
and if both sides you never see
You don't know what it meant to be free.

Lighthouse

Written for my sister and mounted on a plaque as a present on her wedding day

When this marital ship is tossed about at sea
you will find that it is not a catastrophe,
though you gaze at stars alone at the wheel
not noticing where you are pointing the keel.

You should not be afraid at day or night
for in the distance, you can see lit bright-
a lighthouse standing on a rocky harbor shore
guiding you back to safe land once more.

This light will stay with you on your boat
and will do more for you to stay afloat
than anything you can throw at the swell
for you know his name is Immanuel.

He'll guide your hand upon the wheel
even when your boat may pitch and heel
You'll not get lost in this foamy realm
if you'll remember God is at the helm.

 Goodbye

Now, at least, I know where I stand—
it's no longer in the air.
Perhaps we can just be friends
unless you don't really care.

No longer hanging on high hopes,
no more stabbing pain in the heart;
or waiting for you to say three words.
Let's make a brand-new start.

Neither you nor I are the only one
to take on this tragedy's blame,
and we felt good when we were close,
so neither of us should feel any shame.

So, goodbye, my friend—what else can I call you . . .
besides, would it matter in a line of prose?
You will know this is for you by these words I write:
Such bittersweet life shouldn't be just for a rose.

No more walks on the beach at midnight, singing loudly;
or drinks to make us drunk enough to even say, "Hello,"
But I'll really miss your smile and your wonderful smell
each time the ocean is rough and our song is on the radio.

Summer

A BEST FRIEND IS FOREVER
To those who didn't forget we were friends, even when I did

Carry On, Regardless
Prospecting Friends
A Best Friend is Forever
Death of a Friendship
Verse to a Friend
Always Third
If I Laugh
Don't Bother Me
Happy Birthday to a Friend
I'll See You in My Dreams
To One Who Inspired
Iron Lady
Desolation
On Survival
In Appreciation
To Susan
River
Broken Arrow
A Patch of Briars
Trinity
Dark Side of the Moonchild
Duck Shit Sunday

Carry On, Regardless

You now say you've found yourself
and you've begun to like this state;
no longer wanting to join the Army
because of problems with your weight.

I guess you missed the years that passed
but dreams of service stayed on your mind
at a camp you found deep in Georgia's hills
was one for which leaders were hard to find.

You'll leave for there while I stay here;
I wished we had time to drink a beer
remembering times we laughed til we'd cry,
then you'd get upset, and I'd wonder why.

Your life has fallen into place;
I see the joy grow upon your face.
Last year's job at camp is yours for sure,
and you found what you've been looking for.

So, now you think you have the answer
and won't go to Georgia after all.
You'll stay here and be a friend to me,
until your recruiter came to call.

You changed your mind so many times,
that you began confusing even me.
I came to wonder each new day,
"What, today, is she going to be?"

Your life, my dear friend, is a merry-go-round;
it spins fast. I'm entangled. I can't see . . .
One day, when you know where you're headed,
you'll carry on, regardless of me.

Prospecting Friends

If you saw me on the street,
would you stop or pass me by?
Would you size up me or my apparel,
which might not please your eye?

Would you not care enough
to discover that in me
there's something worthwhile
that to some, is hard to see?

Some would say that everyone
on this Earth deserves a chance
to be considered as an individual
and given more than a passing glance.

If you are one of those
let's share our varied lives,
and know a lasting friendship
until our parting day arrives.

So, next time you pass a person by,
pause and take a second look;
a dear friend may wait just inside,
of that stranger you mistook.

A Best Friend is Forever

"A best friend is forever,"
she said to me on the phone.
"Just because I'm leaving the state,
doesn't mean I'm leaving you alone."

"I'll write, and we'll talk real soon;
I'll come back some future day,
then we can laugh, talk and sing again;
we'll always be close this way."

A best friend should be forever;
an ally who never lets you down,
or leave you without a word
when they move from town to town.

They are there to give you comfort
and will try to ease your pain.
Have a few laughs and drinks with them
and still they won't drive you insane.

A best friend is forever . . .
Oh, damn! How would I ever know?
I've never really had one, I guess.
So, alone through this life, I go.

Death of a Friendship

People said we were close—two peas in a pod.
The concept of "friend"— isn't it odd?
Knowing when to share and hear what is said
without probing too deeply and leaving it dead.

Mutual memories that hid emotional pain;
we ran across hills and sang in the rain.
We shared thoughts, dreams, even our tears,
enjoying a special closeness all those years.

I don't know, I can't say what truth is anymore;
you murdered that when you walked out the door.
Did you have to do that without telling me why?
I'd still welcome you back—give it another try.

Your vanity hurt the love of a lasting friend,
who'd support and help you 'til the very end.
You've killed all the others, where'd they all go?
Am I the last surviving ex-friend you know?

Verse to a Friend

It was a cold Tallahassee day
when I realized why I need you most.
I was walking in a graveyard,
talking with a friendly ghost.

The sky was gray; the trees were bare,
but the thing I remember most that day
were the fleeting thoughts of you;
I said them aloud and they flew away.

It's your quiet concern, your belief in me,
and rowdy days filled with laughter;
times we expressed hopes, dreams, fears,
and our loves from here ever after.

In times of need, you eased my mind;
by being there, you let me know
it's nice to have a friend like you
when your thoughts and ego are low.

So, it's you and me, my dear friend,
though we differ, we've shared a lot.
And we will change throughout the years,
but we won't fail if we give-way somewhat.

Always Third

On this expanse of earth we all,
into some repentance fall.
We seem lost within the confine
of something we can call divine.

Divinity can barely be defined
to me, you see, I'm not that kind.
So, don't expect too much of me,
for I am of a different breed.

Ghosts of my past may cause you alarm,
but they are dead and mean no harm.
I keep the memory alive as a reminder token
of events in my life that can never be broken.

They are bound as one by a continual learning,
without which there'd always be a yearning
to know, to have, to see, to feel . . .
that is what makes life all the more real.

I once fell to false sincerity,
so careful now, I'll always be.
So, are you friend or are you foe?
Sometimes, I think, I'll never know.

You say you can understand my thought.
Well, how can you be quite that adroit
at seeing into my dark tunnel of dreams?
You will never hear my silent screams.

You know I want to be friends with you
but I can't do some of the things you do;
only I can approve of me and my past.
You can't stand in the shadow I cast.

You say you want to free my soul?
Oh, it's just fine having its own goal.
Do what you must; go spread the word;
and then I'll know I'll always be third.

 If I Laugh

I feel alone with all these people;
they make me ill at ease.
I can't do the things I want to,
nor say what 'ere I please.

They give me dirty looks sometimes,
and make me feel alone;
but to only one or two of them,
am I drawn to or even known.

There are strained relations here
and things I don't comprehend.
Some people I don't want to know —
they want to be my friend.

Others I'd like to be closer to,
don't see the need in me
to be myself, whatever that is,
without the third degree.

"Why this, why don't you that?"
Tell me how to run my life!
Damn you! Can't you see
I live by the pen and knife?

Why must you inflict your views
on those of us who are in-between?
What makes you think you have the answer;
what do you know that I haven't seen?

I'm not all right, yet I'm not all wrong;
nor a robot am I either —
programmed to do only certain things
and get caught up in silly blither.

So, if I laugh when you say your piece,
I may seem only slightly amused;
I laugh, yet I cry for you deep inside,
as you are more than I am, perhaps, confused.

Don't Bother Me

You left me again, all alone
and I had to wait for my heart
to come back to me and join
my emotions, which you tore apart.

I don't want to see you again,
nor hear anyone utter your name;
I don't care how you are
and I won't play your ridiculous game.

I'm fine now, no thanks to you,
when you left without any word;
don't come to me with apology,
don't tell me you felt so absurd.

Don't bring me flowers or candy,
don't write, and please don't call.
Don't dare pretend you cared, my friend,
don't you bother me at all.

Happy Birthday to a Friend

What can I give to you dear friend,
that would capture fond memories
of those days we spent together
where I felt so much at ease?

I wanted to give you a part of me,
not some knick-knack from a store.
Since what you see here is what I am:
a lot of simile and metaphor.

I'm glad you felt you could unleash
parts of you that you keep private;
for it put you in a different light;
one I thought you'd never fit.

I want you to know that our friendship
will always be close to my heart.
And on this special day for you,
special wishes, before we depart.

Happy Birthday! Lots of love and luck!
What you'll be shows in what you are.
You'll have the universe well in hand
if you hitch your rocket to a star!

I'll See You in My Dreams

It was a cold, grey day when I left the city;
I was all alone and felt self-pity,
for I knew I'd never see again
those who became so close as friends.

I was alone on State Road 27;
it was beautiful, almost like heaven,
but, those fleeting memories . . .
ah, how they came back to me.

> "Come see us again, since we are such good friends."
> But, I know the only way is I'll see you in my
> dreams.

All those college days will bring back a smile,
and we may laugh again when we reflect awhile.
How we loved each other for our unique ways
of meeting the challenge and passing the days.

Should we forget those days we shared together,
or start thinking they were too burdensome,
we should be sad for leaving them behind;
they're only growing pains we had to overcome.

> I know that you're there, and I know that you care.
> But, I know the only way is to see you in my
> dreams.

If we were to get together again,
it would not really be the same;
one may be a success in business,
another let down by fortune and fame.

And so, my dear friends, we were what we were,
but, we all have to say "Adieu"
and I could never put into words
how much happiness I wish for you.

    You were all so kind; I'll always keep that in mind.
    So, I know I will, forevermore, see you in my
    dreams.

To One Who Inspired

To whom I write this, I must say goodbye;
I wanted to thank you and I wish I had tried,
Your ironclad confidence showed me the way
to finding the same for myself someday.

Time erases your image yet not your ideals;
you were admired for winning—you know how it feels.
But you should follow your heart and set yourself free.
Spread your wings—fly—become who you'll be.

You know, in recent times, your mood seems changed
to unhappiness—and priorities became rearranged.
Where had you lost (I wondered with a sigh)
that spirit of warmth, or when did it die?

I once felt close to you, I now draw away;
I have to work hard at something to say.
I want to recall you as sincere if I could;
you were much lighter then, I knew where I stood.

Everything changes much too rapidly now,
but I thought you were immune somehow.
I know I shall miss you and wish you well;
I hope you find happiness wherever you dwell.

Hopes and dreams give a lot of comfort to me;
I keep friends filed away, so alone I won't be.
I'll keep your memory and in time grows more fond
and look back where you were—then go beyond.

Iron Lady

I keep writing: I don't understand, don't understand
how you can ruin a career with the wave of your hand.
Yet a career down the tubes is not what you see
but a favor you did for the Air Force—and Me!

Your halo slipped when my dream was gone
and thanks to you, I'm alone to carry on.
Stop! Look around, iron lady that you are
what do you see, just a third silver star?
Is that all there is—is that all you want?
Under the iron is a loner who puts up a front.

Do you "owe your life to the company store?"
The more you give, makes them only want more.
Goodbye, goodbye, I need not know any more;
it is best that I leave now as I head for the door.

Desolation

Wonder where my friends went,
or rather, should I care?
For those who are mere acquaintances
can't stab me with probing stares.

Now I'm out again in a crazy world,
small and unknown, yet still free
from restrictions set by stereotype,
and I can be what I want to be.

So, those who probed and analyzed,
still don't know quite who I am.
They can't neatly categorize me,
and they know I don't give a damn.

There are those who like my company;
really like it, ain't that unreal?
They take me as I am, you see,
and don't try to feel what I feel.

No one can of course, *no one* can,
no matter how close you are to them.
Don't let them see too deeply into you,
since it gives them more to condemn.

What is this elusive animal: *friend?*
What's the trait of the breed?
Someone who cares, shares, dreams, schemes,
and who'll help you in times of need?

They can't always; I know that of course,
they have to take care of themselves.
Should they put themselves in my hands,
they'd be lost on my dusty shelves.

So why this feeling of desolation?
I guess I feel they all deserted me;
They didn't. Damn! I know they didn't.
They had to, for themselves, break free.

On Survival

Stop all the mind games and become a human soul.
Relate to your friends, without being so damn droll.
Feel like no one reaches to you, you do all the reaching?
Do not go to a preacher, he is much too busy preaching.

Are you alone with all your thoughts—no one talks to you?
They could feel much more, but there's naught they'll do.
Feel like crying, yet no one will touch your tears?
You draw into a ball, for you cannot relate your fears.

Too much ratting going on
and back stabbing going on;
too much lying going on
and too much crying going on.

You can't stay together when people fall at your feet;
don't bleed for old friends; too many new ones to meet.
They'd take from you 'til there is nothing more to give.
You reach a point where all that's left is only just to live.

How can you sit there and think a friend will last forever;
if you never are alone, then you should never be together.
Don't wash away in their wake; go on with what you do.
Look hard into their eyes—not a damn thing's there for you.

Too many braggarts goin' round
and laggerts goin' round;
too many sleuths goin' round,
and not enough truths goin' round

The question, you then ask, is "What is left for me?"
or "How can I live with this friendship denial?
Walk alone with pride, others soon fall into stride,
then you have learned the fine art of survival.

In Appreciation

Who plucked me from my inner fears
    to make me see the golden years,
then gave a smile when smiles were few,
    and encouragement to help me through?

Who slammed the desk to rant and rave
    at all my moods that were very grave.
Who talked to me, instead of *at,*
    and called me very simply, *Pat?*

Who demanded more than I thought I knew
    about what I had learned—my point of view;
or gave me hell when I lost sight of a goal,
    who because she cared, began to cajole?

Who stayed late with me, long after hours,
    and taught me to stop and smell the flowers
because life is short, and they won't always be there,
    of them, you should always be aware?

To teachers and coaches from grade one to degree,
    you've given a lot of knowledge to me.
So, here's a small token of deep appreciation
    for the time, you spent giving a great education.

To Susan

You are a friend; they're hard to find—
you always cared, yet, spoke your mind.
You often probed deep, made it bleed;
(I forgave you; there was a need
to re-open the wounds that never healed—
let it flow, so it could forever be sealed.)

You listened, you heard, that's hard to do;
you never disagreed without thinking it through.
I never felt aware of the span of our years;
after all, laughter is laughter, tears are tears.
And no one, any time, can ever bring an end
to a bond, close enough to be called, "Friend."

River

You were a river, meandering, searching
for a level of living, I once understood.
I was a sandy bank, gritty, stalwart,
who tried in vain, to stop the flood.

Once in a while, you lapped against me;
I hoped you would stay for a while,
but you changed into a laughing brook,
and darted away while I forced a smile.

I dammed you up to stop your eroding me
with all your ins and outs, ups and downs;
and your changing daily, which angered me—
your smiles turned too quickly into frowns.

I smiled as I watched you run your course
and was sad when you began running dry,
leaving me alone, now just a sandy dune,
and I had no more tears left to cry.

Well, I suppose you'll be back someday,
but you'll find the riverbed has changed
and you may not want to run along
something now completely re-arranged.

Broken Arrow

You were as straight as an arrow, clean and true
and I often wished I were more like you;
your courage to go on was admired by me
or at least that was the way I thought you to be.

You never hurt anyone until you had them alone;
your front came down and you then truly shone.
Nail them to the wall, old girl, or they'll get away,
then they can't come back to get you another day.

Yes, straight as an arrow, so clean, so true,
but that little façade didn't last too long for you.
I'm the one who saw right through it all;
you made me angry, cutting me down so small.

Your metal tip melted, feathers came unglued,
while I smiled at it all on a day I had rued.
Your wooden shaft warped and just before it broke,
I heard the last of the false words that you spoke.

No longer special, just a woman with a fault;
some haven't yet seen this and continue to exalt.
But soon they'll open their eyes and will see
that you'd do the same to them as you did to me.

A Patch of Briars

We galloped through the countryside
and jumped over farmers fences;
I misguided my buckskin mount,
and was knocked out of my senses.

I landed in a patch of briars,
and I was angry with you
for laughing at me sitting there;
I'd never seen you from that point of view.

Soon I was laughing with you;
you got down to help pick them off,
making light of my unfortunate plight,
that at first, I thought was a scoff.

No uncertainty remains in our friendship;
we help each other out of various mires;
things I never thought much about before,
and I owe it all to a patch of briars.

Trinity

You never met each other,
but all were so dear to me;
each unique in your own way,
now together for eternity.

We were friends so long ago
that of each other, we lost track.
But the wonders of social media
brought all three of you back.

I always hoped we'd get together
but that was never meant to be,
but I got to hear your voices again—
my special heavenly trinity.

Dark Side of the Moonchild

When the moon is in the fourth house
and the sun is behind the moon,
you will begin to see a change in life,
and you'll be married very soon.

You will have a tiff with an Aquarian
on a sunny July morn,
It is best that you don't marry him—
you'd do better with a Capricorn.

Don't get out of bed tomorrow,
it will be a rotten day.
You'll not get a damn thing done,
you'd better do it all today.

Travel is in the stars for you,
but don't go on a trip;
wait until the summer
or else you'll get the grippe.

This will be your year
it will have sadness and then hope.
Life is crazy but I've begun
to get tired of the horoscope.

Duck Shit Sunday

I don't recall, but I think it was Carol
who named the day, "Duck Shit Sunday,"
but four of us had to get away for awhile
and left mid-term studies for a fun day.

We went out riding in Barb's car
through the Tallahassee hills,
and spied a little pond with ducks.
"I'm stopping," said Barb, "I've had my fill!"

We walked around the pond,
which was shaded by big trees;
we enjoyed watching swimming ducks
and just taking in the breeze.

Lisa spied a little island mound;
I said, "Lets explore this newfound land."
She nodded, and we waded out to it
and discovered it wasn't made of sand.

It was a mound of leaves in the pond,
and I said, "These leaves don't smell light."
It dawned on me and I said, "Oh shit!"
And Lisa said, "I'll bet you're right."

Barb and Carol were bent with laughter,
taking pictures of us on the sandy bank.
They'd known what it was all along
so we laughed with them at their prank.

We got back in the car and found another pond;
got out and started to climb the trees
which were adorned with Spanish Moss;
while we played with it, it made us sneeze.

We finally decided, with the sun in the west,
that we should head back to our Alma Mater.
We got back to campus, but not farther than the gate,
for that was not the end of our playing in water.

The fountain out front of the Admin building
looked like a good place to rinse, so 'round we swam.
Professors came out, looked at us as if we were all nuts —
Well, we were! It was during mid-term exams!

Autumn

IN MEMORIAM
Dedicated to the memory of all in nature that has been violated, trampled, and otherwise forgotten

Paths
The Undefeated Ocean
Destiny
Night Harbor
Painting of a Storm
Storm at Sea
Serenity
Early in the Morning
Sky Beasts
Tragedy
Souvenirs
The Lonely Traveler
To Evening
In Memoriam
Keep On Growing
The Park
Ode to a Canary
Destiny of Frogs
Sunday Morning Tragedy
The Fiend
Sleeping Earth
Boomerang
The New Season
The View from the Porch
Uncomfortable Repose
Patterns

 Paths

Paths to follow, trees to climb;
forests enchanted, life is divine.
What do they teach you, where do they go?
Follow them all until you know.

Sounds of footsteps, fast . . . now slow;
what abides there, how does it grow?
Curiosity lingers like glistening snow;
thoughts march by, row by row.
Where does it lead you, where does it go?
Seek it, find it, then you will know!

The Undefeated Ocean

When ere I see a whitecapped wave
about to crash upon the shore,
I rush to meet it, big and brave
and brace against the sandy floor.

"I dare you! Knock me down," I say,
although I knew it'd be repeated,
since, still unto this very day,
the ocean is undefeated.

Destiny

Earth was once an empty place
where nothing lived or grew.
Time passed, which changed its face;
from the sea came life anew.

Fish spawned, birds took wing,
flowers bloomed—a lovely thing.
All life here had greatly shone
'til mankind made it all his own.

No place on Earth did man not seek;
sailing seas and traveling far
across the land to the highest peak,
leaving behind him a jagged scar.

With fellow men, great wars were fought;
hunger, disease and death were brought.
So careless was the human race,
that again, Earth is an empty place.

Night Harbor

Towering dock lights burning bright,
pierce the shadows of the night.
Water lapping at man-made banks
and thudding boats on mooring planks,
break the silence of the dark.
A phosphorescent silver shark
glides through the water, void of man;
searchlights dance over a concrete span
of a towering bridge, reaching high
into the inky-blue evening sky.
Long shadows fall from shipping crates
and all the silent harbor waits
for darkness of the night to flee,
and dawn to break across the sea.

Painting of a Storm

Thunder rolls in the distance
and echoes through the air
like a toll of death, ringing deep
through my senses, feeling despair.

A swift breeze shakes summer's leaves
in warning of an oncoming gust.
Swift torrents shoot from blackened skies
brim-full with a stormy, chilling lust.

A slashing bolt shoots through a tree,
rips holes in grass and slushy dirt;
rain uproots plants and drowns insects,
while stormy dominance begins to assert.

In time, clouds relieved of their burden
dissipate as the storm starts to cease.
Gentle sunlight caresses soft clouds
in hues gentle as gray doves of peace.

On tips of leaves, raindrops are jewels;
birds once hiding, now welcome the sun.
Dragonflies flutter from grass-blades to trees
as afternoon's rebirth has begun.

Sheltered and dry, I sit at my window,
watching colorful new rainbows form,
jotting down notes of what I just saw . . .
a verbal painting of a storm.

Storm at Sea

In breezes brisk and chilled, breakers roll inside out;
angry waves and whitecaps toss flecked foam about.
Gray clouds bump and billow have overlapping reach,
blacken the wave's wet fingers, groping for the beach.

Then the heavens open, and lightning rips the sky;
rain pours down like showers of sparkling silver dye;
wetting sand and jetties, shining dark and tall,
while tiny rivulets expose the deluge of the fall.

As soon, the storm is over, small wavelets pat the shore,
a ray of light disguises the raging storm before.
Beams of sun spread slowly, giving clouds gold majesty,
casting a brilliant pathway across a peaceful sea.

Serenity

Small ripples of pale blue water
reflecting a cloudless early dawn sky,
lap against my stilled rowing scull
in which I sit, for tired am I.

An expanse of water surrounds me
nudging green grass near the shore;
a gentle breeze caresses my hair
where all was still a moment before.

All is hushed but docile waves
and a rustling of shoreline trees.
The rising sun paints the bridge
a golden hue with dexterous ease.

Its splattered image creeps through palms
and across the peaceful, clear water
reflecting the sun's rays like a mirror
and shine on a lone, swimming otter.

Beyond are fishermen quietly waiting
amid a mixture of ducks and geese.
All gaze across the still lake;
there is no sound . . . only peace.

Early in the Morning

I crept slowly from my cozy, warm bed
and threw open my easternmost portal;
the sea beckoned me and made me feel
that to join it would make me immortal.

I ran to the waves to accomplish this feat,
but, being one with it seemed out of reach.
After many more tries, I grew tired;
returning weary to sit on the beach.

I sat on moist sand watching sunrise
under a chilly, graying sky;
sea spray splattered my face,
while above came a gull's lonely cry.

A bright sliver of gold on the ocean's horizon,
sunrise changed the murky sea's mood.
Glints of fire sprinkled the ocean's expanse,
while pelicans soared, searching for food.

As the flame-colored disk gradually rose,
the water slowly turned fluid gold;
caressing cool sand, light reached the shore
casting shadows in hollows dark and bold.

As I rose to leave, I turned to the sea
with a long last look I needed to give.
This superb event daily, if they might see,
is enough reason for any mortal to live.

Sky Beasts

I sat beneath a tree
    staring at clouds up high
and watched the lofty sky beasts,
    gray and white float by.

I saw dogs chase a fox
    through a cotton field,
and when the sun shone 'round them
    a marvel was revealed.

The sun's rays formed a lion's mane
    around one giant billow;
and made a fearsome head which
    laid down on a pillow.

A parade then marched above me
    of little ducks and hens,
followed by a flock of sheep
    escaping from their pens.

A group of seven horses
    trotted with a sudden gust;
I could almost hear them whinny,
    "Come and fly with us!"

For many peaceful hours
    I watched this show so gay;
then the wind, like a giant hand
    swept the sky beasts all away.

 Tragedy

Cool breezes flow by where I sit
on a bench facing Suwanee Arcade.
I could fall asleep in this lush green place,
at peace in its dense, dark shade.

Moss hangs in front of me like icicles,
in shades of dusty gray which blend
into the vibrant sprouting greens
and blooms 'round the campus I attend.

New Frosh, their parents and siblings
bring back a smile as I remember
the first time I too, saw this place:
it was in summer, not September.

Which means that those here presently
are seeing it as I did then. Now
beautiful and peaceful, early on Saturday.
Fall brings football's rowdy POW-WOW.

It also brings tension and headaches
from exams the Frosh don't foresee yet.
When they do it, won't be flowers or trees
they see—only constant mental sweat.

They'll be inside in air-conditioning
hearing no birds, just the drone
of an instructor. They may wish to doze,
but instead, stay awake with a moan.

They will soon hurry between lectures
with record speed because the next class
is on the other side of campus;
they won't notice flowers as they pass.

They won't see browns of winter change
to spring colors since they'll be busy talking
of physics, chemistry, or whatever they must.
Needing cars will destroy the joy of walking.

Souvenirs

Paddling on a lake that emptied in a river,
I passed a single snake, a slithering sliver.
While floating on this stream of time,
I could see the flora bud and cyme.

I felt alive and high like a bird in flight;
my eyes never saw a more glorious sight:
the sky was so blue it made me weep;
I store this feeling in memories deep.

I'm at peace with myself, all conflicts abated,
I know my thoughts won't be debated.
I'm as free as my stream or a rose growing wild—
I'm a drifter's daughter, yet nobody's child.

The soft breeze foretells a gentle rain,
that sprinkles down then begins to wane.
Creatures emerge from hiding places,
beginning again their frolicking chases.

It's solitude that now comforts me;
time spent under my favorite tree,
letting my mind simply float away
saving souvenir thoughts for another day.

The Lonely Traveler

Weary grow the gypsy's eyes that seek elusive shores,
and tired are the groping paws that test unyielding doors.
So helpless seems the quest for refuge, but access is denied;
endless is the wandering when there is no place to hide.

Empty is the odyssey that knows no journey's end;
desolate the wanderer, spanning worlds he can't befriend.
He trespasses graveyards where no welcome is implied,
in search for offered shelter or somewhere else inside.

Futile, his unyielding search for non-existent care;
tired are his bones and shaggy is his hair.
Massive is his hunger in his soul so vilified.
Where can such traveler run to—where can he abide?

To Evening

Shadows flicker, rush away;
darting, fleeting in each new day.
A full moon and a gentle breeze
bring salt air wafting across the seas.
A mom calls, "Tommy, please come home."
Starry nights under a dark blue dome
inspire twilight summer barbeques,
with firelight in its changing hues.

Young lovers first kiss then stare,
each hoping for the other's care.
While scared kids under covers hide
and toss in bed from side to side.
The moon at which the dreamers gaze,
will fade into a morning haze.
This is evening, dark and deep;
a time of wonder and of sleep.

In Memoriam

    The tree wept.
Some might say it was only water coming up from wet roots
to give nourishment to a dying trunk,
slowing the inevitable death inflicted by one with an axe,
who parted limbs from its base.

    The tree wept.
Many do not think of a tree as a living thing,
but something to covert what we exhale to provide air,
or worse, a landscape decoration to help fill up our yards
and nothing more. (Nothing more?)

    The tree wept.
Because as I remembered good times I had in that tree,
the shade it provided, the protection I felt,
and I won't forget, though it was uprooted and left to rot,
for it was my playground when I had the urge to climb.

    I wept.
Because they said it was a relief not to worry about roots
coming up in the plumbing or cracking house walls,
and that it had no feelings, it was just a tree,
and nothing more. (Nothing more?)

But I know the tree wept,
for it was my childhood friend
and I was the bearer of the axe.

Keep On Growing

Take me back to those old dirt roads;
I don't care how far or where we go.
Their tracks linger deep in my mind
that may only be a refuge, though.
If all those places I love are gone,
then in my heart, they shall live on.

Take me away, I can't bear to see
them tear down my old high school;
their progress makes my mind spin fast,
leaving but a blur for this old fool.
They paved the sandlot where I used to play,
made into a parking lot, pot-holed and gray.

The nation must forever keep on growing
or it will be forgotten for its deeds.
Memories of the past are shot to death,
and then cast among the weeds.
Will you help in turning the tide about,
or will we keep on growing 'til we all die out?

Take me back to those old dirt roads,
I don't care how far, or where we go.
Times were simple then, were they not?
But there was time for character to grow.
You can't build with concrete before using only tin;
how do you advance if you don't see where you've been?

The Park

This park is loved by everyone,
after all, it was planned that way . . .
clipped grass, trimmed shrubs, edged paths—
It's quite beautiful, wouldn't you say?

There once was a dump under all that lush grass;
it was ploughed under to make this park—
a beautiful place to sit, jog, picnic,
skateboard, or make love in after dark.

Before the dump stood, there once were woods
ploughed under to make the dumpy stink—
a place to throw out tin cans and old Raggedy Anns
A very useful purpose, don't you think?

No one who sees this beautiful park
can think back to when it was only a wood.
They like it clipped and sheared to perfection,
after all, it's part of the neighborhood!

But I'll go to the woods in my mind every time . . .
unless you want to make a park out of it!

Ode to a Canary

Yeah verily, we lock you in cages,
then wag through the bars at you with a finger.
Were you to wish for anything at all,
you'd wish for quick death—that is your freedom!

Debt owed to you will soon be paid;
and indeed, to all nature we have encaged.
As we imprison your kind, so have we ourselves,
confined our true freedom until nothing is left.

Darker, darker, grow the clouds of time,
so we vainly war with it as it advances.
We look back, longing for days gone by
and blindly mourn the canary, happily singing!

Destiny of Frogs

Thunder roared,
and lightning flashed;
a tree fell down and
a frog was smashed.

On a rainy night
when motorists rushed,
there was no time to see
a frog getting crushed.

Nearby, two boys
catch a small green prize.
They can't resist poking
out the poor thing's eyes.

As sad as it is
it seems to me,
These varied fates
are a frog's destiny.

Sunday Morning Tragedy

I was just fifteen that awful day
when I heard my stable buddy say,
"Don't throw stall ten his feed or hay,
Tiny Horsefly died today."

Tiny was a pleasure horse
who sometimes ran a barrel course,
and who you never had to force.
Tiny Horsefly died today.

When Tiny's boy, naively cruel
entered his beast in a deadly duel,
he gave its life to the youthful fool.
Tiny Horsefly died today.

The racing course was a five-mile stretch;
other nags in the match, he couldn't catch,
and was left on the track, a broken wretch
Tiny Horsefly died today.

Two weeks later a man agreed
to buy poor Tiny, a lamed-up steed
not knowing rest was his only need
Tiny Horsefly died today.

The man then took the aching horse
and entered him in a barrel course;
giving death for Tiny its only source.
Tiny Horsefly died today.

The creature screamed and kicked in pain;
his eyes and tongue were bulged insane,
dragged away now at the end of a chain.
Tiny Horsefly died today.

On a Sunday morning, clear and cold
inner wounds in me took their hold;
at age fifteen, I became quite old.
Because Tiny Horsefly died that day.

The Fiend

When the weather's hot and dry
people simply won't go outside;
they might as well go die,
as they stay inside and cry.

When the weather's damp and cold
they stay inside and start to mold
from cold and clammy wet—
they've not learned a damn thing yet.

There's a writer in the house now;
oh dear! A writer did you say?
What will all the neighbors think
about one who writes and gets no pay?

Just a case of cabin fever, Doc?
Everything's going to be all right?
Just a temporary bit of insanity—
what'd you say—don't turn off the lights?

Not 'til the writer goes out into the sunshine
and leaves the typing alone for awhile
and starts acting normal again, oh well,
you'll know if she hears a bird and smiles.

Sleeping Earth

My heart does not rejoice now
when leaves are turning gold;
for autumn turns to winter
and preludes months of cold.

A flashy show of bravado—
like one who hides their fear;
then showers us with color
but knows dismal days are near.

The trees are sashed with scarlet,
the meadow is frosty white.
A waning sun shines sadly
on migrant birds in flight.

I sit beside the fire,
content within its glow;
outside the earth is sleeping
beneath a new-laid snow.

Boomerang

I had a little dog whose name was Boomerang;
no matter where I went, I'd call and up she sprang.
I took her everywhere with me, even to the park;
whenever she was happy, she let out a happy bark.

I named her as a puppy when I found her near the track,
she'd always run ahead of me then she'd come right back.

She was a sandy brown, bright eyed little scamp
who pranced and danced around, always played the vamp.
She'd wag her tail as she followed me there and here;
getting into all sorts of things—she never did know fear.

She was killed by a car one night; I guess the driver didn't see;
and I know she's up in puppy heaven and barking happily!

The New Season

Young deer stalked through golden leaves
while chipmunks scampered 'round.
A noisy jay called for friends to flee,
since frost was on the ground.

Clouds were piled gray on gray;
the ground was cold and bare.
Trees no longer held their leaves;
an icy chill was in the air.

Children hurried home from school
as snow began to fall.
Ice was crunchy underfoot,
though the amount of it was small.

Young deer stalked through golden leaves;
while chipmunks scampered 'round,
noisy jays were heard no more . . .
for snow was deep upon the ground.

The View from the Porch

Sitting on the front porch, rocking in chairs
at the end of summer—it is blazing hot.
Is that a fall breeze, rustling through our hair?
Nope, just the ceiling fans so I guess it's not.

They keep the biting skeeters off our tender skin
while we sip lemonade, watching folks go by
who will wave, say hello, or at least give us a grin.
They might come up to chat or shout out a "Hi!"

Here comes the Lord of the Manor with a glass of wine.
So named since he has a golf cart to get around.
As he talks, we see an enigma who's so hard to define;
His baby boy is crying, and he wants to escape the sound.

Another guy across the street works a job he cannot stand.
On one side is a professor who will walk her dog and wave.
The widow on the other side still wears her wedding band;
She drives into her garage, closes the door like it's a cave.

We enjoy our porch more when there's a natural breeze
And less of smelling the automobile emission-ing
The skeeters get too bad for the fans to bring us ease
and run us off our porch, into the air-conditioning.

Uncomfortable Repose

Silently, snow falls and covers the ground
in a white blanket, crunchy underfoot.
Clean, crisp the air, snow, fresh and wet;
absent of a big city's smoke and soot.

In mountains high, where peace reigns supreme
and wild beasts roam, no cars honk—what a pity.
Since I am not used to nature's silent repose;
it's too lonely here, I'll return to the city.

Patterns

Rain drops fall one by one
   into a pool of water
and form bulls-eyes, which ripple.

Sun's rays diffuse through
   the big oak tree's leaves,
caressing the ground in shadows.

Snow falls on a roof, then melts,
   running over the edge
freezing into bulbous icicles.

Sand in desert shift in hot wind
   settling into shallow hollows
as a gritty undulating sea.

Wind whips around big rocks
   and carves its deep mark
leaving behind stony statues.

Fire dances in the moonlight
   in a friendly campsite
licking the air with its red tongue.

Winter
PROVERBS OF MY SEASONS
"The wit of one and the wisdom of many."

I hope my wit is worthy of the wisdom of the many who have preceded me.

A Lifetime
An Old Song
Wisdom of Water
Mountain of Truth
Woodard's Garden
Alone in the Dark
I Looked Away
I'm Going to Neptune
Life in a Goldfish Bowl
Old Woman of the Road
Prophesy
Silence
My Soul and the Wind
Drift Away
Like Dreamers Do
After Work
The Savage
Graduation
Beware the Grapevine
Memories
Paper
Fighting the Same War
Island in the Sun
Pipe Dreams
Poetry
The Child
Ascension
Pulitzer
Advent

A Lifetime

Never a worry, never a doubt;
never thinking of what they're about.
Cheerful and frolicking children at play
lead the same life through each new day.
Then time takes over and steals from their eyes
the beauty of fields, pastel painted skies
and birds in green meadows. Instead puts there
deep-set looks of new worry and wear.
Late years advance, summer days gone forever—
they can't help looking at youngsters together.
The sweet wine of youth almost drained from the cup,
the continual wish they'd never grown up.

An Old Song

Blurs of children skipped among
shadows of a sunlit route
and fading like a lilting flute,
left behind a tune half sung.

Silent, the day had lain
before turning dusky gold—
someone passing, hunched and old,
sang the last, abandoned strain.

Wisdom of Water

We are but ripples
   in a pond
      when a rock is thrown
therein.

The ripples will soon
   fade away,
      in waters still once
again.

Mountain of Truth

I cannot see far today—
a veil enshrouds my sight
so, the peak to the mountain of truth
seems as dark as night.

Instinct wills me to seek the summit,
but I stumble through the fog.
I cut my hands on jagged rocks,
wearily stumbling to sit on a log.

Bewildered, yet determined, I go on,
to continue climbing toward that peak.
My weapons are confidence and hope
to lift the veil of truth that I seek.

Woodard's Garden

At Woodard's garden, I go to think
of how religious culture has undone
potential for peace to serve as a link
between nations under the Holy One.

I ponder wars fought in the name of God
midst trees and blossoms by the pond.
I wonder how far Christian soldiers trod
to reach the land of the great Beyond.

The birds here sing their forever songs
in unison with buzzing bees,
ignoring religious rights and wrongs,
innocents playing tag around the trees.

Some beliefs claim to be the only way
and will save your lost soul in the end.
Their disciples dole out pamphlets by the ton.
"Here's what you seek, you can depend!"

I want no part of their rigid ways;
they all claim to search hard for the Grail.
Mother Mary, have you seen better days
when it was more than room for their ale?

I believe that God is the spirit of life;
and stays with you while you're living—
a lifeforce, part of every action you take,
bringing joy to the simple act of giving.

There is a thorn tree in this garden, though
here to remind me not all in the world is well:
Some take beauty for granted and tear it apart;
but in the garden, I find peace for a spell.

Alone in the Dark

People on this planet are lonely and crying.
In spite of living they do, they really are dying.
Some live deep within their walls of illusion
seeking answers to questions they ask in confusion.

There are too many now, crowded and huddled;
searching for control of the lives they've muddled.
They think money is key to immortality,
but instead, it brings them early fatality.

Look at them, with lips that utter not a sound,
and eyes that do not see for they never look around
at the sorrow and tears of another's pain untold—
all that is left is a heart grown hard and cold.

Wandering aimlessly through life, alone in the dark;
forgetting simple things: laughing brook, tiny lark.
They are dead within themselves, unable to touch
the person next to them who may need it so much.

Seeing only themselves in the dark of their mind,
they shun the light, afraid of what they'll find.
They cry out, beg for help to someone unseen;
proving only, they need a crutch on which to lean.

When the end is near, fear shows the way
and opens their eyes, ears, and minds in one day.
Oh, but now it is much too late to hear that lark—
once again, they find, they are alone in the dark.

I Looked Away

Hush, hush, Oh damn you, hush!
You'd better pray I will not rush
and make a mess of both of us.
Oh, stop! Shut up, you crazy cuss!

Whose idea was this anyway?
You say they'll miss us both someday?
Won't that be nice—all so grand?
But we'll never know under so much sand.

Why don't we both have change of mind?
Life can't be all that unkind.
I've had enough of this suicide,
I think I'll find a way to abide.

Get away from me with that knife,
I said I want to go on with life.
Why don't you give yours another try?
You'll accomplish nothing if you die.

She threatened her life in spite of me,
playing a game of "chicken," you see.
Since she wanted me to regret that day,
she stabbed herself, I looked away.

I'm Going to Neptune

I'm going to fly to Neptune
just to leave all this behind—
this annihilation of the earth,
reversed progress of mankind.

These blocks of brick pile higher and higher
and remind me of a funeral pyre.
They won't be on Neptune, nothing's there
but peaceful water and clean, icy air.

I won't simmer in a summer city's pot
filled with dive bars and loud guitars,
or get lost in swarms of human faces,
no longer choke on smoke from cars.

Nor get lost in parking lots and malls,
smell dirty water as it runs from pipes
to form the sewer, that rat oasis,
agleam in the midnight streetlights.

I won't see false love in humanity,
where they smile their smile and let you be.
Nor see tall buildings painted black with soot,
to collapse on children underfoot.

On Neptune, I won't ask, "Who am I?"
There's a place for all you see . . .
Oh, I do hate to quit the human race,
but I've got to find a place for me.

Life in a Goldfish Bowl

Circling 'round and 'round,
never getting anywhere
for all my expended effort,
until outside, a leap I dare.

But, outside may be insecure
and people hard and cold.
If alone and free, I could be,
I might be more daring, bold.

An occasional oak would be
on my dreamland's soil,
where I'd dream my lazy dreams
or maybe just rest from toil.

But, alas! I can't foresee
that place in time for me,
so, I'm stuck here in this goldfish bowl,
left to drown in life's debris.

Old Woman of the Road

I met on the road, a woman one day,
whose form was hunched and old;
the many things she told me
were worth more to me than gold.
Her face was etched with deep lines of life;
while smiles held laughter, eyes mirrored strife.

This wonderful and aged tree,
who was dried, brown verdancy,
had much color left in her voice
as she conversed with me.

I asked her why she was traveling
this road she'd seen before.
She said because the first time,
she'd gone too fast to know its lore.
She set the world ablaze in her younger years
but no wisdom was gained from passionate peers.

Yet, she did not preach to me,
or say my pace was wrong,
nor try to slow my growth,
for she knew my life was long

I started this road too fast, but now it's undertaken,
I must slow down, and as she said, I should reawaken
myself to think hard on this life. As I watched her fade away;
I may not see this road but once; I walk slower since that day.

Prophesy

All your life, you are taught to have a role,
if not lived, can make you seem less whole;
without dissent, you must fit into their mold,
and with your voice, do not ever be too bold.

Then you are sent far away to learn,
yet in your heart, other dreams may burn.
Those who teach, still see their hearts in you;
at one time, a desire burned there too.

But at school, you must put away your dreams,
and be conditioned to life's daily screams.
And while you're free to speak your mind;
you may become like the others: dumb and blind.

And when it's time to leave the guarded fold,
it will be time to go into the public's cold.
Until then, they will teach you all they know,
and one day, they will tell you, "You must go."

For in your life, there is so much work to do
and one day, others send their young to you.
Then there's a need to teach them all you know,
for someday, you must tell them, "You must go."

Silence

Silence is where there are no screams
   or bloodthirsty schemes;
where there is a cool, gentle breeze,
   yet, no rustling of leaves;
where there is no maddening confusion
   or the grand intrusion
of people who are so well meaning,
   coming at you, faces gleaming.
Silence is a gray, misty fog
   hovering around a bog;
and silence is a joyful dream . . .
   coffee with the richest cream.

My Soul and the Wind

I looked out my window and all I could see
was a wild, silky darkness which called out to me.
Then, from my heart's chambers, from deep inside
my soul seemed to answer, and for freedom, it cried.

I walked through the darkness, not knowing why;
feeling new sensations—like I really could fly.
As I walked through the wind, at last, I felt free
from my constraints, finding deep parts of me.

Then came the morning, I lay buried in thought
of my night with my spirit and what we forgot.
My soul and the wind are rejoined at last,
and my days of unsureness are now in my past.

Drift Away

Am I a happy corpse?
Oh no, not at all!
Almost happy while living,
then the end came to call.

I could never reach a peak
in actions or words I speak,
of profoundness to suit my ego;
at this moment I feel quite low.

I've too many lies yet to resolve;
too many books and verses to write,
too many friends to find or lose,
but I can't see them without my sight.

Just as I began to find out who I am,
a voice from the grave beckons me.
Aren't I still a bit young for this—
I've too much to do, can't you see?

I've not done a thing for humanity,
just getting done with teen insanity;
there's supposed to be more than tears
from now until the final years.

Well death, be quick, don't linger long;
don't crack a joke and don't sing a song,
for I've not had my chance to sing,
to laugh, to love or any earthly thing.

I haven't said all I want to say,
nor can I say it in a single day.
I'm quite let down by life all in all;
come later, Reaper—or better yet, call.

But I won't die from my own hand,
even when I'm old and gray;
I won't have them fit me with that brand;
But I won't just simply drift away!

Like Dreamers Do

They say a dreamer lives forever,
but I know that's untrue;
a lifetime spent on casting dreams,
I do like dreamers do.

I dream of love, I dream of hate,
and of things which may seal my fate.
I dream and simply contemplate,
like other dreamers do.

I dream of things that won't be resolved
unless all humanity gets involved;
yet, all I do is dream this dream,
like a dreamer is apt to do.

My only goal is thinking
of questions there are no answers to;
never swinging into action,
I do like dreamers do.

Only wondering of things I might try.
of love and happiness I might give.
So, it's true a dreamer never dies,
for they never really live.

After Work

After work, I have a few;
it always tends to change my view
to something a little more rosey.
(or daffodilly, tulipy, or posey-ey!)

And do you think I should regret
having my whistle all gleamy wet?
Why no! My muscles go into repose
and the rest of me may start to doze,
but, what do I care, I'll start to smile
as I dream of being out of the rut awhile.

When I wake to do it all over again,
adding days to the years of my twenty or ten,
I can do it quite well, with a little smirk
as I await my time, after work.

The Savage

Turn me onto the dark and dreary
before I'm too old and too weary.
Let's see all they call the human race
before I vanish from this planet's face.

Take me down to murderer's row,
now that would be a marvelous show;
show me addicts, pushers and boozers
and all those other grand-scale losers.

Take me where the red lights burn
and let me watch you take your turn.
Show me babbling men lying in the gutter
with an empty bottle, they can only stutter.

Take me to see some occult witches
who turn their seances into riches;
show me how the blind can lead the blind
in religious cults which steal your mind.

I am a savage, yes only a savage—
a human, that's me! How much life can I ravage?
I have no feelings—can't afford feelings;
I live only for me, and all of my dealings.

You can call me lover or call me friend,
but I hope you remove all the knives in the end.
So, turn me on, then tune me out,
then at least I'll know what life's about.

Graduation

I but look around me in panicked desperation,
trying to seek something I should have seen before.
I wish you well my friends, but it only brings frustration,
for I do care but I shouldn't since it won't matter anymore.

I see their little exodus from the barracks to the gate,
all smiling and proud of their trite accomplishments
that they truly do believe are those which seal their fate,
and feel their feeble beginning is their precedence.

I see a hundred accomplices to murder of human feeling;
they became so brusque thinking it makes them tough.
But all it did was make them apprehensive of a smile,
they began to complain about the training being rough.

I see foes that could be friends and friends that could be foes
but, to neither could I give enough time to finally know.
So, they leave here now with soupy eyes or angry brows
that soon will disappear, for all they wanted was to go.

I watch them toss their hats and begin to break formation,
all chattering and happy now that it's all over and done.
They soon will forget the words they swore with dedication
to the life which they have chosen yet, it's only just begun.

Beware the Grapevine

Beware the grapevine, its fruit is sour
and should make the bravest of you cower;
meddled information, just passing through,
nothing useful that you'd feel a need to outdo.

A glass snake in the grass is all that it is,
shattered to pieces—each a new hiss;
once shattered, the pieces all come alive,
to be a new courier to spread all the jive.

Beware the grapevine—Beware! Beware!
Continue to listen, you'll be caught in its snare.
For soon, you'll find yourself on the vine
as fast talk flows as quickly as wine.

Memories

Today is a day of memories...
Spring brings rebirth after a long, cold winter
bringing with it a change in mood,
and remembrance of past sad-to-happy times.
Memories are like that, shifting with seasons.

Remember your friends from years ago?
Where are they now?
Wonder where she is, what became of him?
Are they happy or in love?
How are they spending this day of transition?

Remember those you worked with last year?
Do they still have their crazy sense of humor
that you thought gave them the guts to press on?
Do you feel differently around them now
and can you remember if they changed, or did you?

Remember if you will, those with you now.
Can you get close to them
and let them love who you are;
and want to remember you?
Or will you pass through their minds, forgotten?

Today is a day of memories... You make them...

Paper

Look at all the paper people
living in their paper-doll world.
Light a match, it's all in blazes,
scorched and all the edges curled.

Have a friend and love them dearly;
it will last a year or two.
They all seem so temporary—
what is in their heart for you?

Open your eyes and see the shifting,
red turning quickly into blue.
Everything around us is moving,
can it be you're changing too?

Don't you see that you are different;
not the same as you once were?
And don't you have to alter also—
fade to blend in with the blur?

Is your cardboard castle standing
and filled with those you love?
You can't keep them there forever—
what have you been thinking of?

They'll break down your pasteboard walls
and won't like your paper chains.
Will your crying keep them there?
Paper weakens when it rains!

I've been searching through my life—
why don't all my dreams come true?
Am I wrong to think I'm different?
Yes! I am made of paper too!

Fighting the Same War

I tried to fit the perfect image
of what a good officer should be,
by filling the squares and dotting the dots,
but it all came much too mechanically.

They ask you if you are good enough
to be a part of their fold;
I began to ask the same of them,
but the stares they gave were cold.

I didn't understand the attitude of
officers to the enlisted—they'd ignore
both new comers and life timers—
hell, we're fighting the same war!

If captains rolled up their sleeves
to help complete the piled-up work,
they'd find more respect for their rank
and sergeants wouldn't call them a jerk.

Delegation of duties is fine and well,
but some get carried away with it all.
"You take care of that, I'm on coffee break,
and if there's a problem, give me a call."

But Lord, when we must come together,
when the enemy threatens our shore,
the damn fools may open their eyes and see
hell, we're fighting the same war!

Island in the Sun

My life is a journey, my body, the ship;
my spirit is captain and impetus whip.
Alas! My ship needs constant repairs,
and being alone, the captain despairs.

Master of the Abyss changed my destiny
and has taken my ship to places not free—
over rough waters way out of its realm,
while I was stargazing, not watching the helm.

Set adrift, it suffered lack of command;
finding its way to uncharted land.
But, by itself it's a mere empty shell,
devoid of a mind, it would wander to Hell.

The captain's not trying to run it aground,
just dreaming of a where good life can be found.
Setting a new course—finally, the right one
that will take her to that sweet island in the sun.

Pipe Dreams

Experience life, savor the flavors;
throw out those that don't taste good.
But to never have known what is there for you,
is not to have lived at all like you should.

Will you watch your dreams swirl
around the room in the form of smoke
from your pipe bought in retirement—
life so empty that now you choke?

Why the compulsion to be somebody,
when this present rut is so cozy?
You already know what life is about
from watching it float by, so rosey.

But you still dream about one day,
being all you can without a fear
of reproach, and to taste life in full,
but you'd rather wait 'til next year.

As empty smoke gets thick in the room
you don't remember your dream, and you pace.
It is no longer real, but it used to be big.
You died with sadness on your face.

Poetry

Thoughts drift through their mind on a breeze,
awaiting the poet to write them down.
But thoughts could be lost forever
if the poet isn't indelible or renown.

Thoughts of love in its most glorious hour
or of times when life that seem most sour,
are first seen in the poet's mind in a dream.
They see and know or that's how it may seem.

They write things only they may understand
for sometimes their thoughts are a fairyland.
They translate them for the world to see
and in case you forgot, that's called poetry.

The Child

What would you do if I gave you wings?
Would you fly with a bird and see why it sings?
"No," said the child, "I'd fly high in the skies,
up to the heavens to see if God cries."

What would you do with all the money in the world?
Would you buy castles, gowns, silver, gold or pearls?
"No," said the child, "I'd give it all away
to my unfortunate friends who live day to day."

Of all the boys you know, whom would you marry?
The rich boy on your block whose name is Jerry?
"No," said the child, "he only knows money;
I'd marry one I love, who is sweeter than honey."

Of all of life's mysteries, what do you hate?
The luck of the draw, which could bring a bad fate?
"No," said the child, "life is taken in stride;
it is part of a great test, so, I must abide."

If you could have anything, what would it be?
A mansion in Paris, a yacht on the sea?
"No," said the child, "I only want peace,
where all the wars at once would cease."

Ascension
Written for my father and recited at his funeral.

He cannot smell a rose,
nor can he feel its thorn,
nor watch its petals unfold
in the early, early morn.

He is at peace, no doubt;
no worries crease his brow.
He'll not cry another tear—
no need for roses now.

Cookies, he'll not taste again,
no more meals will he prepare;
and if you have a favorite dish,
he is happily unaware.

He may still be with us
in every thought and deed;
But, just remember one thing
his pain is forever freed.

He can't hear you speak kind words,
or know how much you'll cry
when you realize how much he meant
he's with the Lord on High!

 Pulitzer

You are a hero now.
They've made you into that.
You are one for the ages
and it matters not that you're alive.
If they waited, it still would have happened;
you'd just be a dead hero.

Back when you mattered
you would have hated this prize.
You'd say it was too establishment
but you are old now and it seems Okay
to add it to your mantle,
to admire in the few years left,
Mr. Zimmerman.

 Advent

Who are you?
I can ask the question, but I can't answer it.
What do you want?
You will know the answer, but only if you ask yourself.
Where will life take you?
As far as you wish, but fear will be an obstacle.
When will you know?
Perhaps at age 30, or perhaps you never will.
Why won't you?
Because you may be afraid of the reality in your answer.
How will you overcome it?
Become a child again, follow dreams, and take chances.

Acknowledgments

I have a lot of people to thank for their encouragement in bringing this to a point where a work like this is possible.

My husband Gary has been encouraging me for years to put a volume of poetry together and I am sure I have frustrated him for the 30+ years that it has taken to get them to this point.

Saundra Kelley is a poet herself, which is why I wanted her to be the one to rip them apart as she critiqued them. Lyla Ellzey encouraged me to keep sending to poetry contests, even after I kept getting nowhere with them. (Still haven't.) Dee Christensen, who read them, said he enjoyed them and told me to "Package 'em up!"

Local poetry groups **Poetry for the Love of It and Big Bend Poets & Writers** helped me see that unrhymed poetry can also be fun. M. R. Street for the suggestion of putting four collections together to make separate "seasons."

To my publisher DocUmeant Publishing, for taking on this project and understanding that a poet's work doesn't need to make sense to *everyone*, but simply that it is worth the effort to get it out there.

Grateful acknowledgment is made to the publications in which some of these poems have previously appeared:

Afterglow, Published in Hearts on Fire

Souvenirs, Published in American Poetry Anthology

The Park, Published in Best Poets of 1986

Thank you!

The author trusts you enjoyed this small peek into her world. She would love to hear from you. If you enjoyed reading this, her first book of poetry, please consider leaving a review and share the love of rhythmic expression. For those of you who are not comfortable using your given name, you can use "Avid Reader" instead.

It's simple to leave a review. Go to your favorite online book store listed below and type in *"Proverbs of My Seasons"* in the search bar.

Click on book icon, then "customer reviews" or scroll to "write a review".

Amazon: https://www.amazon.com

Barnes & Noble: https://www.barnesandnoble.com/

Goodreads: https://www.goodreads.com/author/show/16549074.Pat_Stanford

Do you want even more?

Visit Pat's website to view her other work, purchase additional copies, and see news and upcoming events.

https://www.patstanford.com/

To book Pat to speak at your organization's meetings, conferences, workshops, or book club email her at PublishedPoetPat@gmail.com.

| pat.stanford.14 | @wordhacker_pat | pat-stanford-33786393 | stanford.pat |

ADDITIONAL WORK BY PAT STANFORD

Fixing Boo Boo

A Story of Traumatic Brain Injury

Retail: $17.49 | $6.99

324 Pages

Publisher: DocUmeant Publishing

ISBN-13: 978-1-950075-08-9 (print)

ASIN: B07VX95SQX

All Barb really wanted was to be treated like everyone else. All the family wanted was for her to be safe and well cared for, especially after a life-changing accident that left her brain-injured. When her husband died, she needed assistance to cope with daily meals and chores.

Her sister and brother-in-law encouraged her to sell her house and come live with them. They had no idea what dealing with brain injury meant. They found out!

Available online and at your local bookstore. Ask for it today!

www.ingramcontent.com/pod-product-compliance
Lightning Source LLC
Chambersburg PA
CBHW070852050426
42453CB00012B/2154